LETTERS

TO

MY PAST

GRACE HEMPHILL

Copyright © 2017 Grace Hemphill. All rights reserved. No portion of this book may be reproduced, stored in a retrieval system, or transmitted in any form or by any means—electronic, mechanical, photocopy, recording, scanning, or other—except for brief quotations in critical reviews or articles, without the prior written permission of the author and publisher.

ISBN-10: 1546875891

ISBN-13: 978-1546875895

DEDICATION

Thank you to my parents for giving me my creativity.
Thank you to my siblings for giving me my passion.
Thank you to my two close friends, you know who you are, for being there for me through this journey.
Thank you to past English teachers for showing me what I could achieve.
Thank you to the one who helped write this book.

Presents

People give me presents, every day.
Some big, some small
I open it up, expecting a gift.
But as I unwrap the paper
I open the unexpected
I carry the unknown in my bag, every day.
It weighs me down.
The more presents I get, the heavier my bag gets
Until I'm on the ground,
Scraping my knees, blood, cuts and scars
It would be easier if I could drop the presents
But once you see what's inside,
You can never forget.
So they will always stay in my bag,
Dragging me down.
Forever, until I get a bigger, heavier presents
That takes up the space.
But secretly my old presents will stay with me,
Smashing me into tiny pieces.

YOU'RE JUST A STUPID
BROWN HAIRED BOY WITH
BROWN EYES SO TELL ME
WHY I AM MORE ADDICTED
THAN ANY OTHER DRUG

graciehemphill.com

Rage

Freedom of speech is a basic human right
But apparently, my words don't matter to you.
Before I even open my mouth, it seems I am wrong.

It doesn't matter what I want, need or desire
because it won't
happen.

You suffocate me to the point I might as well be
dead.
I live in a cage.

You've locked the doors where can I get the keys?

Am I meant to stay as your slave until I'm no longer
useful.
I want to live.
To feel what others feel.
Instead all I feel is enclosed.

I get you're protecting me but how do I know what
you're
protecting me from. I want to experience.

How will I survive if I don't know what it looks like
outside?

These 4 walls no longer interest me and I'm sick of
waiting.
Waiting to feel happy about being here.

You write so beautifully, the inside of your mind must be a terrible place

graciehemphill.com

Too Little, Too Much.

Someone once asked me,
What makes someone so evil?
And I said,
Too much hurt, not enough plasters.
Too much hatred, not enough love.
Too many people throwing them about,
Like they're not worth anything,
Too many dreams shattered, like 7 years of bad luck. Too many tears, not enough tissues.
Like a massive storm that makes the boat tip over,
Being forgotten,
Misunderstood,
Used,
Too much spare time in that one familiar room,
Where the walls hold your secrets, cries and screams,
Too many scars from the battle.
Not enough attention.
Not enough care, like a newborn baby.
Who's too fragile,
One drop and it's damaged.

One time I came home from school, shut myself in my room grabbed the scissors and frantically dragged the blade across my arm

graciehemphill.com

Grow Up

I feel trapped in my own house.
Who I want to be, isn't who I should be.
But who I should be, isn't what I want.
I don't like making decisions but I don't like you making them either.
Mummy, when can you let me grow up?
I've served my sentence.
Now let me go.
Please.
You don't have the right to control me.
I'm not your robot.
If I don't explore the world.
I won't know what perfect is. I won't know what you want from me.
Every time I make a mistake, you drag me down in the dirt.
Who made you Miss Perfect.
Who made you decide I was shit at life.
Who made you a monster.

I used to tell him everything and he pretended to care

graciehemphill.com

Love

I'm not   sleeping. I've
stopped eating.   For My brain
is too full. And my   stomach. Has
grown small.Thoughts   of you. Block
My vision. Like   walking through a
fog. And I can't see   where I'm going.
You don't deserve me. You think
I'm like the rest. Far from it actually.
I'm just too damaged. When I don't hear
From you. Irrational thoughts flood
My head. Why do I worry? When
You're not even mine? Love
And obsession. Makes
Me emotional. You
Not believing me
Makes me
Cry.

Don't you love me? don't you want to show me with the act of making love, how much you love me?

Second Chances

Do I let you suffocate me again?
The world states what doesn't kill you makes you stronger but does it?
Am I strong enough to handle it a second time?
Or am I strong enough to realise I don't need to go through it again?
Have you changed at all?
Am I going to risk it all?
For you to say the words I hate, for rejection.
For laughter but not my own.
Please say you've changed.
Please don't rearrange thoughts of you in my head.
Please don't play a board game where I already lose because I'm weak.
And you cheat.
Please be as blunt as a pencil.
Please say these jokes aren't going to turn into reality.
I don't want to ask.
It's just a doubt.
Medusa had a doubt and look where she is now.
I don't want to be a monster.
I just want to know the truth.

He used to be everything you thought you wanted and now your life has turned into a nightmare that you can't wake up from

graciehemphill.com

I Want You

I want you,
Like a fading patient needs its new organ.
But I can't seem to walk away,
When the situation gets red-blooded.
Your rope is round my neck; restraining me.
When I walk backwards.
It aches.
I can't grasp the knowledge.
Do you want me to be content?
Or am I your next hunt?
Your psychological relief,
As you watch my unconscious mind bow down to you.
I crave you.
Like a drug addict devours their heroin.
But I don't want; dried up tears and day old bruises.
I avoid being lonely.
No matter how purple my neck goes,
You are worth the screams and cuts.
You may not be the plaster I need.
But you'll be the distraction.

I fancy you,
Like a writer lives for their paper.
If I abandon you, I cannot go on with my daily life.
I get stressed out.
There have been so many times I have wanted to give up.
But no matter,
How messy it gets,
I won't rip you up.

"I waited to ask you out till you were 16 so I didn't become a registered sex offender" he said. The only way he could be more blunt was if he had said "I want to fuck you until I get bored and then leave you"

Skinny Girl

"I've already eaten"

she says.

The girl sitting across the table.

Looks down, still not content with who she is. She gets stares.

From those who dare to look.

She told them not to worry.

"I'm becoming good enough"

She says.

Beauty is in the eye of the beholder,

But no one gives her the time of day to notice.

Attention she craves.

From anyone who wants to care.

Even if they don't.

Even if they don't care.

It will be good enough for her.

She's just empty.

Within a blink of a eye he pushes me against a tree, with his hands down my jeans, I had no control over the situation

Shattered Pieces

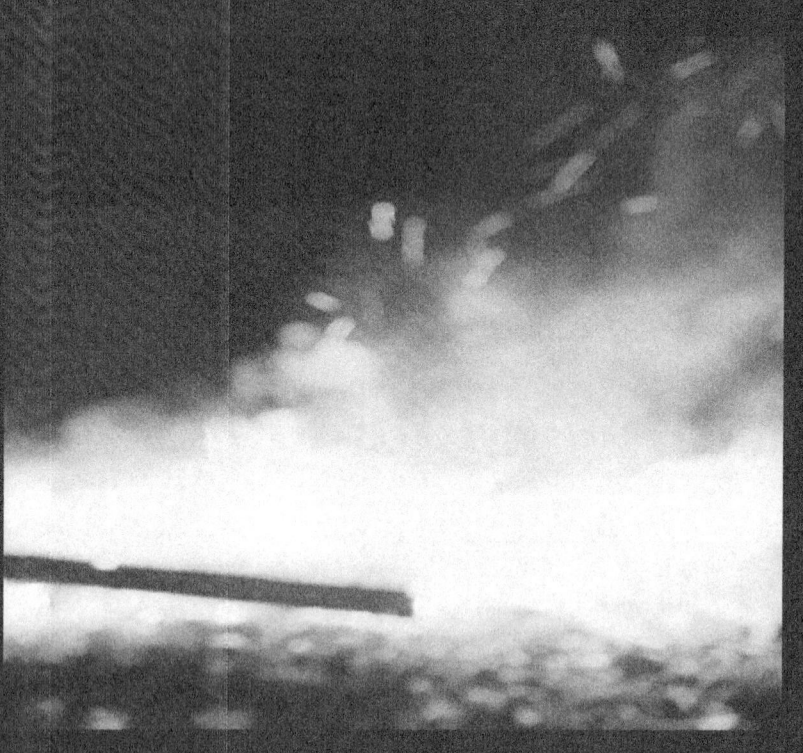

I feel   Broken, like   A mirror.
Your disgusted look you give me,
Says   It   All.
You're never happy with how I look
You   Seek   Perfection   In   Me.
And become disappointed when there's
Nothing   There.
I feel bad for how I've made you feel.
I try to tell you you're beautiful,
But   You   Still   Cry.
It's like I'm silent and it doesn't matter,
What I do. I can never make you smile.
You hold   In flaws,   Make   A goal.
But   You   Always   Compare.
You scream at me,   Blame Me.
It's not my fault. I'm sorry I'm not what you wanted.
I try to show you what everyone else sees.
You   Think   I'm a   Liar,
You throw objects at me, I deserve the pain.
One day I'll break underneath your pressure. Then
You'll   Be   Sorry.

You broke me yet I was the one apologizing

graciehemphill.com

Feeling Blue

Infant children.
Pretending to be something; imagined being superhuman.
How old to you have to be before that game doesn't work?
End of the day you still end up in bed.
As the pitiful, pathetic girl in your head.
"Pretend to be happy and you eventually will be"
That's what they said.
But it isn't working.
I don't have the imagination.
To trick my mind into feeling any variation.
You tell me.
I have to be fine.
I have everything anyone could ever want,
How can that make me so weakened?
Nothing makes me content anymore.
Does that make me unappreciative?
I'm disorientated.
And I need you to believe that I'm not lying. It's not something you can see, like a wound or a bruise,
But it still destroys me.
Don't ask me to explain it.
The chemicals in my brain can't work out if I deserve to be feeling this way.
I just do.

Once you have broken
the plate it doesn't matter
how many times you say
sorry it will never go
back the way it was
before it met you.

graciehemphill.com

My Guilty Pleasure

The voices in my head.
Telling me I'm better off dead.
You're with them, chanting my name, putting the others to shame.
You push me down. Making me drown.
You having fun there? Stripping me bare.
The sadistic tone in your voice, it's like I had no choice.
I had to suffer, to be in pain. For you it was some sort of gain. You treat me like shit and I used to just go with it.
Not anymore. You may have won this battle, not this war.

She tells anyone and I'm breaking up with you

I'm Trapped

I walk outside
The ice wind captures my voice, crawls up my arms
Across my torso.
His arms tighten
Around my stomach.
I can't move. I'm trapped.
I feel his bittersweet breath.
On my neck, behind my ear
It quickens, he tightens more
I. Can't. Escape.
I try to speak, tell him to go
Leave my mouth.
Why won't he leave me be?
I can't scream for help
I clench my fists.
Open my eyes.
And he's gone.

As little girls we are
told that if a boy is mean
to you it just means they
like you. And you just
liked me right?

Where To Go

It hurts,
Like I've swallowed broken glass
And every time I breathe,
It slices my heart.
No one sees my pain
They assume I'm surviving.
But there's only so many tears,
I can cry.
So many hugs,
I can receive.
And so many love songs,
I can put on repeat.
But then what?
Once I've done all I can
And it still kills me.
What do I do then?
I could follow the demons,
That seem to drag me down me down. Each and every time.
Or I can move on,
And try to pick up my broken pieces. And see if anyone is willing,
To fix me.

Stockholm Syndrome: I'd still adore you with your hands round my neck

graciehemphill.com

Doors

Adrenaline kept me up at night, it was dark.
The only thing lighting the room was my blindly bright phone screen.
You don't understand how you made me feel,
That night.
You promised me you had changed.
But you were still the same person
You were a year ago.
Shame on me for trusting you.
I told you things I tend not to whisper.
But you didn't care.
Not about me.
I was open
But you closed that door, trapping my fingers.
I don't think you understand,
What pain you put through.
You turn to look at me and smile.
Like everything's fine.
But that boat sailed a long time ago.
I smile back,
Pretending it doesn't bother me,
So your ego doesn't get boosted
By me caring.

This is one of those stories you have where afterwards you think of all the other things you could have done.

graciehemphill.com

Trains

Standing.

Cold wrapping his arms around me. Waiting.

I feel their stares on me.

Paranoia pretends to be my best friend. Time goes so slow, eerily slow. Earphones in, forget it all.

I cross the line.

I feel the wind as it speeds past me. Hit me.

Just hit me.

graciehemphill.com

I was there to comfort him

Hugs

That moment when,
I'm close to breaking down.
And from behind his giant arms wrap, Round me.
And for a split second.
I'm fine.
Not the fine you tell,
Your loved ones.
Not the fine,
Where you secretly hope
They notice you're not surviving. This fine is better.
But once the arms go,
So does part of you.
Leaving you more broken,
Then you were to begin with.
Who knew something so good, Could make it worse.
Your angel goes to leave,
And that's when you realise,
You're not strong.
Or brave.
You're just a crumbling cookie. Waiting for a disaster.

I wanted to tell him to stop but it was as if my mind and body weren't connected. I could see what was happening but I couldn't do anything to stop it

Friends?

I miss him,
I miss the way he used to care.
The way I was the single most important person to him.
Now I'm the last on his list,
In the back of his brain.
How the tables have turned.
I didn't need him to begin with,
And now I can't have him.
Why do I care?
It shouldn't bother me,
But it seems it does.
The ants crawling up my legs,
Seem to be giving me more attention,
Than him.
I can't waste my time getting upset,
Over someone who won't get upset over me.
He probably doesn't even realise.
And I want it to stay that way.
I'm glad he's happy.
Seems I was just a temporary fix.
Till he found her.
You just fucked off.
Thanks for being everything,
You said you hated.

For everything you promised you wouldn't turn into.
He walked out on me whilst,
I was mentally slitting my wrists.
He gave me the rope
And closed the door.
It seems I am too complicated for people.
Feeling too much or not enough.
I'm not entirely sure,
What people want from me.
Part of me trusted him,
Part of me saw this coming.
And yet it still surprised me.
I didn't care.
But he made me.
So god damn much.

He found me annoyingly frigid

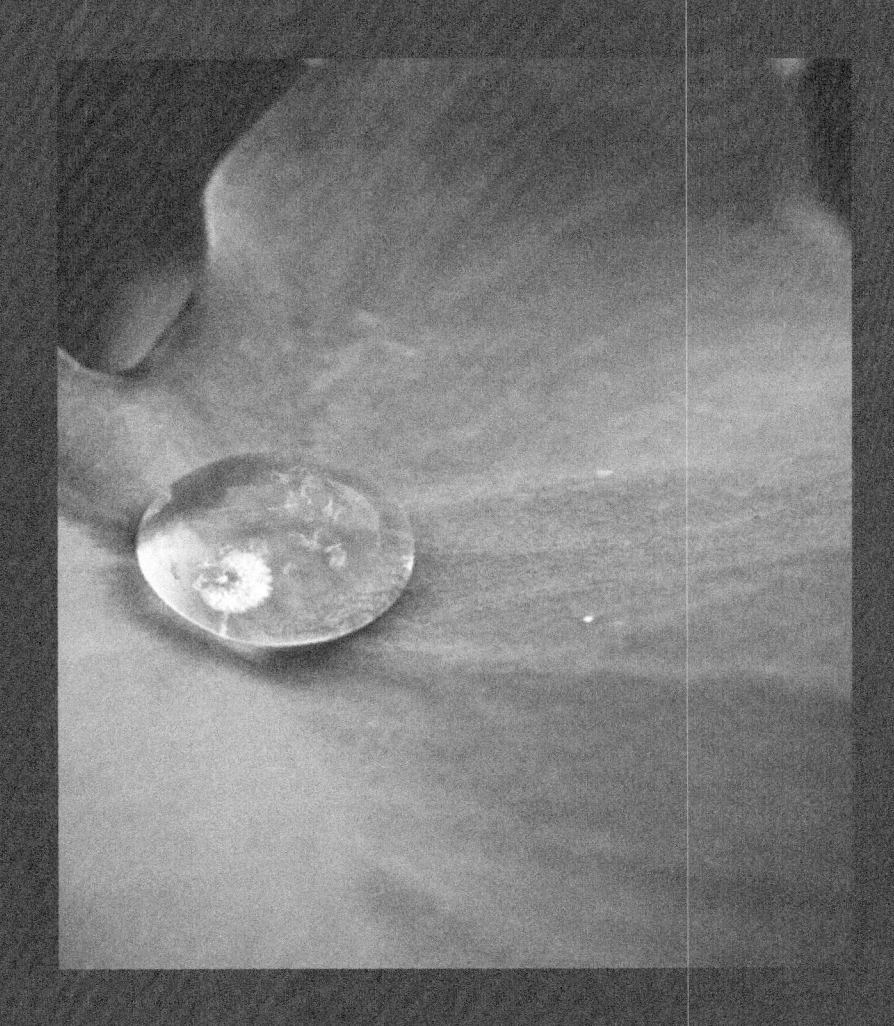

graciehemphill.com

Poison

I drink it to feel real. Alive.
It doesn't necessarily make me feel better just covers up the reality I live in. Too much makes me sick. Just enough keeps me awake.
It's a psychological need. I could live without it but I don't want to.
I want to be so close to death that it ends up staring me in the face.
I take risks.
Hoping danger comes with it. I'm unmotivated. I want to be gone.
But I don't want to do it myself. Someone just give me a bullet and shove it in my chest already.
I thought life was going to be carefree. I don't remembering signing up for this. My head is overcrowded with so many intoxicated thoughts, that don't even sound like me.

Before we do anything
I want to just admire
your naked body

graciehemphill.com

Thoughts

Tears rush down my face.
I don't know why either.
I've had enough. But still haven't had enough.
It's meant to get better.
That's what they tell you otherwise the world would be a quiet place.
You want change, sick of the same old routine.
You used to be strong but that got worn away.
You now just exist.
All the good things they said would happen.
Haven't.
You subconsciously inhale the bad and exhale the good to speed up the process.
Your nails become knives, digging into your skin.
It makes you feel better.
Away from the hell of reality.
Away from it all.
It allows me to runaway whilst staying completely still.

I knew he was no good for me and was making my life miserable but every time I thought of leaving him it hurt more

graciehemphill.com

Realism

Emptiness.
Is all I feel.
My heart isn't even beating.
I can't hear.
I feel numb.
For that split-second I feel carefree and then it is back to hell. I want to go back.
Back to the dark place where nothing feels real.
Where you have nobody's expectations being shoved down your throat.
Where you don't have to care what people think.
Where emotionless is a feeling.
Where not knowing who you are isn't a problem.
Where I can sleep forever.
My hands keep on shaking.
I just want someone to save me before I drown.

Deep down he knew what he was doing was wrong

graciehemphill.com

Your Victim

You're on my mind all the time. You're properly mental.
But I adore you all the same. Though you are judgemental.
Some people don't understand. They just see my bruises.
They never believe I'm ok.
Think it is me he uses.
I think of you as I walk home. Footsteps. I hear noises.
I go to run after, I see it's you. Then my heart drops and destroys.
The dark figure in the distance. Grabs my hand and takes me.
I don't have time to feel anything. Or even disagree.
Your eyes tell me secrets for now. But your hands hold me tight.
I can't even escape this hell.
Not even for tonight.
Trapped in your arms as your victim.
You are brainwashing me.
I can't be enjoying myself.
I think, tied to a tree.

His sharp knife caresses my neck. I know it's all
over.
My eyes shut for the final time.
I need a four-leaf clover.

I had a perceived inability to escape

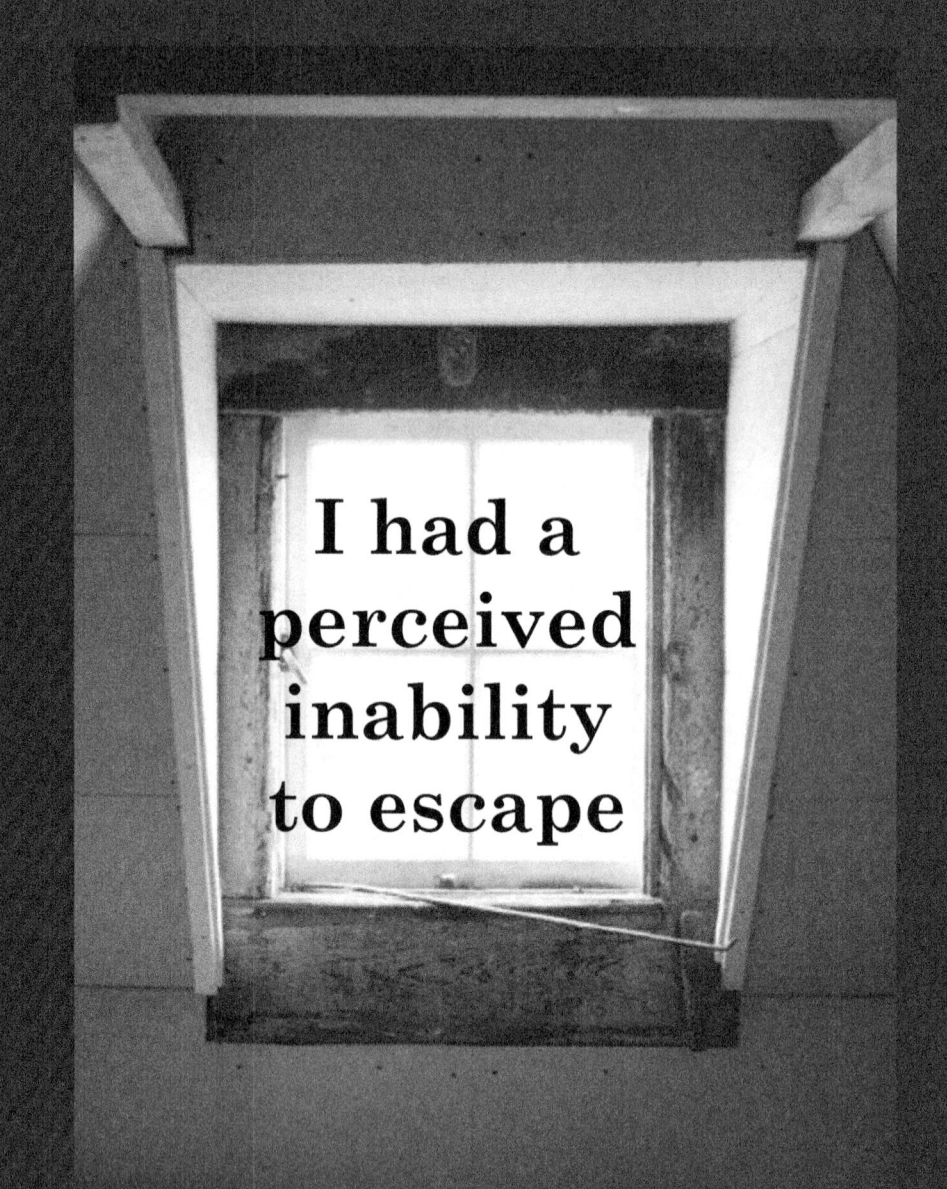

Rainy Days

You know you're fucked when those 1am thoughts,
Start to appear in the afternoon.
You were starting to believe what your parents said about you; You are just an ungenerous, ungrateful child.
All you do is think about yourself.
Do something for someone else once in your life.
And I did.
I gave him my world for I felt that was how much he was worth.
And there were moments where I think he thought the same. But something changed within him.
He changed.
Maybe he had demons like me.
But his were narcissistic heart breakers related to the devil. Once his needs were met I was no longer necessary.
But I loved him.
I didn't care I just wanted to be with him.
Even if that meant crying my eyes out as soon as I got home. Vodka became my best friend.
The strong kick to my throat hurt.
But not as much as him.
He told me he wouldn't hurt me. Yet he did.
He told me he wouldn't leave me.
Yet he did.

Dear Past Lover

You're the reason I cry at night.
The reason I desire to be alone,
Drinking.
The reason I blast my ears full of depressingly true words.
I have no confidence in anything I do.
I'm scared of failing,
Disappointing.
You're the reason I can never trust a single soul again.
I let you in. Into my naïve heart.
And you ripped it.
Because you could.
I can imagine you sitting, thinking, laughing about what you did.
You gave me warning signs I couldn't see.
You broke me yet I'm the one apologising.
You're the reason for the late night google searches,
On how to forget someone.
Forever.
I want to tell people but at the same time I'm ashamed of the secret.
You used me.
Abused me.
And whilst I shiver myself to sleep every evening,
You don't even remember my name

ABOUT THE AUTHOR

Grace Hemphill used to write fictional pieces as a young girl but now spends her free time blogging and writing poetry. On her blog, she writes opinionated topics on a weekly basis at www.graciehemphill.com. Her poetry tends to revolve around abuse, depression and suicide, however she has written poems based around different topics before.

Gracie is the middle child out of her five siblings; she has an older brother, two older sisters and two younger sisters. Being part of a big family she felt she had to stand out to get noticed.

This book is her collection of poetry which she wrote in her late teenage years.

Printed in Great Britain
by Amazon